Rules of Engagement

A Professional's Guide to Self-Defence Law

Will James

First published in Great Britain by Lawful Survival Ltd
This first edition released April 2021

www.lawfulsurvival.com

"The power of the Lawyer is in the uncertainty of the law."

-Jeremy Bentham

For HM-S

Contents

Rules of Engagement

In security circles, the apparatus of the law — police, solicitors, courts — has a name: The Second Enemy. If the first enemy is the violent offender who comes to do you harm, the second enemy, many professionals believe, is the legal system, which may seek to punish you for whatever you did to defend yourself. It is certainly true that the process of investigation into violent incidents is viewed by many with great distrust and apprehension, and this is largely because the whole apparatus is shrouded in mystery; few in the security or self-defence industries have a solid grasp of how it works.

It is as if, in the self-defence world, everyone from professionals through instructors, all the way to beginner students, believe that the process of law is a game of chance that no one knows the rules to. As if you just have to do your best and stay alive through a violent incident, and then face the Second Enemy when it comes, armed with no more than a prayer that all will be well and you won't go to prison.

There's even a saying, "It is better to be judged by twelve than carried by six."

Better you act first to defend yourself and end up going to prison than not fighting back and getting killed by a violent offender.

But what kind of choice is that?

It doesn't have to be this way. If you're a martial artist or self-defence student, or even a violence professional who faces violent offenders daily for a living, you will have dedicated many hundreds of hours to training and development, in order to learn physical intervention techniques that give you a chance to survive, and even thrive, in the physical conflict. Why can't you do the same in a legal sense?

I'm not talking about being a lawyer. You don't need a law degree to navigate the dangerous waters of self-defence law. You just need the right information and the right understanding to go along with your physical training.

That's what this book is about. It is a field guide to the law and its processes as they relate to use of force and self-defence. In these pages you will find everything you need to know about legal process, so that you can protect yourself legally just as you train to protect yourself physically. This field guide is intended to provide you with a complete, fluid understanding of the law in the United Kingdom surrounding use of force. It is a summary of the Rules of Engagement section from our definitive self-defence book, Lawful Survival, presented in a concise format that will fit in any duty bag, and it is supplemented with a wider selection of scenarios and fictionalised examples to assist you in your learning journey.

This book also provides the perfect accompaniment to our Rules of Engagement seminar series, and is a complete reference of all the material we teach during those events.

Welcome to Rules of Engagement, by Will James and Lawful Survival.

Module 1 – Neither Judged by Twelve Nor Carried by Six

No study of self-defence or close-quarter-combat is complete without a study of the law that surrounds use of force in self-defence in whatever country you live in. A fluid understanding of the law and its processes will not only help to keep you from falling foul of the law, but will also help you to make moral and responsible decisions about your use of force, and teach you to question these decisions ahead of time to be sure you are acting in defence of life and not in defence of ego. This applies to both civilians and professionals. No professional is above, and exempt from, the law surrounding use of force (although police are permitted certain actions and justifications denied to a civilian).

It cannot be stated enough that self-defence is the use of superior violence against the violent. To use self-defence is to inflict harm on another human being up to and including the taking of life. Every action taken in violence is potentially lethal, right down to a single punch or a shove. People fall over, they bang their heads, they bleed, they seize, they die. In a live, violent incident, you are only ever a movement away from having your life taken, but you are also only ever a movement away from taking another human's life. You owe it to yourself and others to be absolutely sure that your actions are just, necessary, and defensible both morally and legally.

But what is moral and legal? What do these terms mean? Are they the same? At its core, the purpose of the law is to hold members of a society to moral account for their actions, but the morality of self-protection changes depending upon who you speak to and what their own personal experience with violence is. It's very easy to walk the moral high ground when you have never been in danger, or have never had loved ones in danger and been forced to make a decision between your commitment to and belief in peace and watching someone do violence to a loved one because you failed to act. Facing violence is a leveller; it strips away a lot of nonsense, a lot of pretence, and cuts right to the core of a person. Children have the same effect; ask a parent what they would do to protect their children and the answer is anything and everything. There is no moral high ground when you're talking defence of your children. Anything and everything. Whatever it takes.

Anyone who has taught reality-based self-protection seriously and professionally will have come across students who come to training with the clearly stated goal of learning to defend themselves, but who drop out of training soon afterwards when they realise the true nature and implicit horror of what is being taught. Real self-protection is violence. Proactive, deliberate violence. The only thing separating it from criminal violence is the context and intent with which it is used. A criminal uses violence to subdue and incapacitate, to gain financially, or emotionally, or sexually, or simply for the pleasure of causing the pain or death of another person. An innocent person acting in self-defence uses violence in the simple, animal defence of life. Same violence, totally different morality, but each in their own way just as horrific and just as incomprehensible to someone who has never faced the mammalian terror of being violently assaulted.

The moral questions of self-defence must be explored ahead of time. You cannot try to work out these issues in the heat of assault, when you are on the ground with someone kicking you and there's a decision about whether or not it's right or moral to stamp through your attacker's knee, crippling them perhaps for life. That hesitation is death or serious injury to the unprepared. You must ask yourself now, in the peace of your home — or in the training hall — what you're prepared to do given various situations, and you have to find an answer.

If you have never seen violence up close and unrestrained, do not be quick to jump to judgement. Yes, there are many steps that one can theoretically take to avoid violence, but there is always a chance, on a dark and terrible night, that violence will be an inch away from your face before you've even comprehended the threat and you will have to act, or be hurt or killed by your inaction.

Is it moral to cripple a man if he has attacked you without provocation and is kicking you on the ground, and there is a good chance that you will suffer serious injury or death if you do not cripple him? Is it not common sense that, because you did not cause that situation, you have a right to act in your own defence and a right to go home to your family?

What right does any violent attacker have to safety, when they visit harm on an innocent? What right do they have to cause harm to you, freely and without resistance?

The law in the United Kingdom, and in many other countries, agrees with these sentiments. The law around self-defence gives the uninitiated a framework for understanding the morality of violence. Most genuine self-defence cases are obvious in nature from the start, by the testimony of witnesses, location and nature of injuries, history of those involved and the presence of CCTV at the incident. Most genuine cases of self-defence never make it to court, and of those that do, few fail in their plea of mitigation. Where genuine self-defence pleas fail, it is often due to a failure in understanding of the victim, a failure to tell the difference between defending life and defending ego, a failure to stop using violence at the right moment, a failure to use verbal or postural cues to demonstrate lawful defence, and a failure to adequately justify actions to police on their arrival at the scene of the incident. We will explore these issues later, but to begin with, if you have no clue about how to approach the dilemmas of violence, the law is a good place to start. How else do twelve people who have never been near violence come to any reasonable, rational decision about whether a use of force was moral, if not by coming at the question from within an established and proven legal framework?

In this text we will walk you through that legal framework, and do our best to make sure you are neither judged by twelve, nor carried by six.

Module 2 – Pre-Requisite Tactical Understanding

While Rules of Engagement is not designed to teach or explore the tactical aspects of violence, it is not possible to understand and apply use of force law without first understanding a small section of vital tactical concepts. This module is designed to teach the pre-requisites that you will need to know in order to get the best out of Rules Of Engagement.

Learning Outcomes:

- You will be introduced to a small selection of vital tactical concepts, without which it is impossible to fully understand the law and its application.
- You will discover the limitations of human reaction time, and learn why these limitations relate to the justification of use of force, particularly pre-emptive force.

- You will explore the Speed of Violence, and discover why control and restraint is not always possible, even for a trained professional.
- You will learn why, even for a professional, it is often impossible to control a violent offender without causing damage to that offender.
- You will learn why running is not always a safe option and why there is a moral, tactical and legal justification, in some circumstances, why a person should not attempt to flee a violent incident and should instead fight.

Media Misconceptions

We will start by looking at the problem. Decades of martial arts movies and television series with dramatic fight choreography have created a number of false beliefs about what a human being is capable of in terms of hand to hand combat and self-defence. If we believe what we see in action films, for example, it is possible, with years of training in martial arts, to fight off tens of attackers with complex techniques, even if those attackers are armed. As fantastical as our entertainment is, beliefs such as this become instinctive and hard-wired, and end up colouring the perceptions of all people, even police, solicitors, barristers and judges.

This colouring of perception leads to a very erroneous idea about what a person is able to do, particularly if they have training on their side. It creates situations where barristers or magistrates ask victims of violent crime who have defended themselves, especially professionals, why they could not restrain the violent offender without causing injury, or why it was necessary to harm the violent offender at all.

To combat such popular misconceptions, you need to understand the tactical and legal arguments that dismantle them. The first such argument we will introduce you to is the argument surrounding the limits of human reaction time.

Principle 1 - The Limits of Human Reaction Time

It is a widespread, almost universal belief that, with significant training, a person can learn to block and counter an incoming attack — such as a punch — reliably. This seems reasonable. However, even this simple belief breaks down under logical analysis:

- Human reaction time (HRT) is well documented. The most common experiment to determine HRT is to get participants to sit in front of a screen displaying a coloured box. When the box changes colour, the participant is to click a button. This experiment has been carried out online hundreds of millions of times, and you can do it yourself by visiting sites such as Human

Benchmark[1].

- Following mass experimentation, such as the Human Benchmark, it is widely accepted as fact that the average human reaction time is a quarter of a second (250ms) for a human to react to a visual stimulus. Aural stimuli are reacted to a little faster (170ms), and touch stimuli a little faster (150ms).
- This 250ms figure is to react to a simple stimulus with a pre-determined, simple action.
- Clearly, it takes longer to make a decision and then act. It also takes longer to lift or move an arm than it does to move a finger to press a button. These figures, then, are optimal numbers. Real life will see slower times.
- Training to improve these reaction times is possible, but has its own limitations. Training for many hours a day for up to six months can reduce reaction times by a maximum of 10%. Further training does not reduce times beyond this ceiling. When training stops, improvements are lost.
- Age adversely affects reaction times. Train for 20 years and you are 20 years older, and slower, your age quite possibly counteracting the advantages you gained by training.
- A punch thrown as fast as possible by a trained individual can cross 50cm in around 30ms.

---

1 Test your reaction time with the world's biggest reaction time experiment.

https://humanbenchmark.com/tests/reactiontime

- Even with training, and youth on your side, your physical limit, in terms of reaction time, is around 170ms for a visual stimulus, which is 140ms too slow. To reiterate, it is scientific fact that no training will change these numbers. This is a hard limit.
- Even unconscious, instinctive reactions — known as reflex reactions — are too slow to stop a punch inside the range of 50cm. In a 1984 study, it was found that the head was the fastest moving of all the body's reflex actions, with a latency of 60-120ms,[2] which is still 30-90ms too slow to stop a punch.

What does this breakdown mean to combative tactics, and to the law that stands in judgement of these tactics?

Primarily, it means that if we are within striking range and the threat throws a punch, we will not be able to stop it landing. If it is accurate, it will land. If it is effective, we will be incapacitated, facing further unchallenged harm up to and including death, at the attacker's whim. No training alters this fact.

It also means that we must maintain a space between us and any person(s) who are presenting a hostile or aggressive threat. Professionals call this space a Reactionary Gap.

---

2 Davis, M. (1984). "The mammalian startle response". In R. Eaton (Ed.), *Neural stop of Startle Behavior* (pp. 287–351). Plenum Publishing Corporation.

Key Learning:

In terms of justification for use of force, maintenance of a reactionary gap is essential to prevent you from being within striking range of a potential threat. If that threat then takes away your space, you step back, then they take it away again, preventing you from maintaining a reactionary gap, then you are moving towards, or have already reached a justification for use of pre-emptive force.

Tactically, it can be said that there is no effective self-defence without pre-emptive use of force.

In many cases, force is justifiable as soon as you are unable to maintain a reactionary gap due to the other party's aggressive forward movements.

The concept of HRT is the backbone of the legal justification for pre-emptive use of force, and is absolutely critical to good and skilled use of force justification.

OODA - A Breakdown of Reaction Processes.

There is a good experiment that you can conduct with a partner at home or in a training environment.

Exercise:

Two participants, A and B, stand facing each other, with no more than 30cm between them. Remember that aggressive attackers will take away space by default, and violence will often be initiated at ranges inside 30cm.

Both A and B start the exercise with both arms by their sides, and face each other squarely. This is a position of tactical equality. In other words, both parties have equal capability and opportunity to attack and harm the other.

A's task is to poke B in a shoulder with the finger of one hand. B's task is to react to A's movement and stop the contact with a block using the relevant arm.

A makes this easier by stating which shoulder they will 'poke' immediately before starting the movement.

Where we have run this exercise in seminars, and in well over 95% of thousands of repetitions, B will be unable to stop the 'poke' impacting the shoulder.

Why does this happen? We have just explored the fact that the limits of human reaction time make B's efforts futile, but what is the mechanism that makes it so? What takes so long, in terms of reaction A's attempt to poke B's shoulder?

In the mid-20th Century, an American Air Force Colonel called John Boyd, was the first to describe a framework for understanding reaction processes under pressure. It was called OODA.

OODA is an acronym. Here it is in the context of our poking shoulders exercise:

- OODA stands for Observe, Orient, Decide, Act.
- In the case of our exercise, B hears a word — left or right — and simultaneously sees A's arm begin to move. Both are Observations.
- B interprets these Observations and comes to an understanding about what they mean — that A is going towards the left or right shoulder, the object of the drill is to stop A, and that this drill requires a block to occur. This stage of the OODA process is the Orientation.
- B makes a Decision — block with the left or right arm, as appropriate.
- B Acts, putting into practice the previous step's Decision.

OODA, then, is a four step process. Problem is, B is on step 1 when A is on step 4. B will always fail, unless a lucky pre-emptive movement is carried out.

This exercise is further proof that action always beats reaction inside striking range.

Principle 2 - The Speed of Violence and Why Control and Restraint is Not Always Possible

We have already stated that most people — prosecutors, jurors and judges included — have a very unrealistic set of beliefs about what is possible — and what is not — in terms of self-defence. From a professional's point of view, one of the most important misconceptions is around control and restraint.

There is a belief that it is — or should be — always possible for a skilled individual to control and restrain a violent person without causing harm to that attacker, even where the individual faces the violent person one on one.

For those not versed in professional intervention, control and restraint means techniques designed to gain control of a person without injuring them, and either hold them in restraint until help arrives, or apply restraint devices such as handcuffs or leg restraints.

Our tactical manual, *Lawful Survival*, deals with the Speed of Violence in detail, but we will summarise the concepts here:

- Every moment of a violent exchange gives all parties an opportunity to act.
- Each action 'costs' time.
- Time, and 'costs' can be simplified into a model that can help us to understand what is possible and what is not possible in terms of violent action.
- Every movement, or action, will take a certain number of 'beats.'
- A punch takes one beat.
- A complex control and restraint technique

takes many more beats than one. For example, there is a technique designed to control the person by gaining mechanical advantage over the arm and attacking the wrist to cause pain. It's called a Gooseneck. This is a staple of police safety training, and is a restraint hold that is highly effective once applied. The problem lies in the application. The Gooseneck takes around 5 movements to apply. Each of these movements takes the same time, approximately, as a linear punch. In other words, it is possible for the violent offender to punch you 5 times in the face before you get control and apply the hold.

- Therefore, it is very unlikely, from a tactical perspective, that a single person would be able to effectively restrain a person if that person offered violent, or *active*, resistance.

Key Learning:

Control and Restraint often requires striking to apply. In other words, it is often necessary to damage the violent offender to weaken or distract them, enabling a restraint hold to be attained. Police trainers call this Distraction Striking.

C&R without striking and injuring the offender is not usually possible unless those attempting the restraint outnumber or significantly outnumber the

offender.

Principle 3 - Why Running Away is Not Always a Valid Solution to Violence

- Some states in America have what is called a 'duty to retreat' clause in their self-defence legislation. This means that you must show that you attempted retreat or withdrawal from the scene before resorting to violence to defend yourself.
- UK law contains no such clause, however, as we will explore later, the more actions you take to de-escalate or avoid conflict, the better your legal position.
- Running, however, is not always tactically possible and can have grave consequences.
- Are you faster than the person threatening you? Would you bet your life on it? How old are they? Are they in trainers?
- Are the people with you — children for example — faster than the person threatening you?
- Where are you running to? If no place of safety nearby, will you run out of steam before you reach safety?
- Can you fight for your life after a hundred metre sprint? If there are multiple opponents, the first only needs to delay you. The rest can reach you relatively fresh, and overcome you with ease.

Key Learning:

A duty to retreat exists in some jurisdictions but not others. In England and Wales, there is no legal requirement to run. If you do run, however, this will still count in your favour if you later use force in self-defence.

There is often a strong justification for not attempting to run, based on the tactical principles outlined above.

Module 3 - Definitions in UK Law

In Module 3, we present the legal definitions necessary to understand and get the most out of Rules of Engagement. Module 3 is a concise guide to all the relevant aspects of the law in the United Kingdom, and will bring you up to speed about all the offences of violence and disorder, along with

Learning Outcomes:

- What is an assault, and why does this definition matter to the legal justification of use of force?
- What are the offences of violence and disorder in the United Kingdom?
- What limitations and guidelines are provided by UK Statute and Case Law, for self-defence?
- What do the terms Reasonable, Necessary,

and Proportionate mean, and how can you be sure you are acting within their confines?

- The Circumstances as You Believed Them to Be - why honestly held belief is a key factor in judging the legality of use of force.

Part 1 - The Definitions of Offences Under UK Law

(The following applies to England And Wales. There are some differences to law in Scotland, although the same rationale applies nationwide.)

Assault

The first, and perhaps most important definition in law is that of Assault.

Many people assume, incorrectly, that an assault is where one person strikes or otherwise physically injures another person, but the term, 'assault' has a different definition and does not require any physical contact or injury to occur for the offence to be 'made out', or complete.

Consider the correct definition:

"Any act where a person intentionally or recklessly causes another person to apprehend immediate and unlawful personal violence."

From this definition we can draw out the following facts:

- Assault has occurred when one person's actions — be they words, gestures, messages, or whatever else — result in another person believing that immediate and unlawful violence is about to be used against them. **For the offence to be made out, it is not necessary for any physical attack or contact to have been made.**
- The violence threatened and apprehended must be immediate and possible immediately.

This definition is important because it will later help us to understand what the requirements are for a lawful **pre-emptive** use of force.

Battery and Common Assault

You may hear Police refer to an assault as Battery, or sometimes as Assault by Beating. This is the physical component of any assault. Where an offender has walked up to a victim and punched them, causing only superficial injury, the offence of Assault and Battery (or Assault by Beating) will have occurred. This offence refers to low-level harm, and is also often referred to as Common Assault. Examples of injuries that would fit this level of offence are:

- Grazes.
- Minor bruising.

- Superficial cuts that do not require stitching.

Assault Occasioning Actual Bodily Harm (ABH)

An Assault Occasioning Actual Bodily Harm is simply an assault where the injuries are more than superficial. Typical injuries that might result in a charge of ABH are:

- Loss or breaking of a tooth.
- Cuts requiring stitching.
- Multiple areas of bruising.
- A simple break of the nose.

Unlawful Wounding / Inflicting Grievous Bodily Harm (GBH)

GBH is a very serious charge. Unlike the lesser offences against the person, GBH charges involve a consideration of intent. Section 20 deals with GBH where there was no specific intent by an attacker to seriously wound the victim, whereas Section 18 deals with attacks where there was a specific intent to cause serious wounding. The sentences reflect this severity; a Section 18 charge can result in a life sentence for the perpetrator. Typical injuries that might result in a charge of GBH are:

- Permanent disability, loss of sensory function or visible disfigurement. Examples: loss of eye. Acid burns or glassing to face. Loss of fingers or toes. Crippling injuries to the legs. Paralysis.
- Broken or displaced limbs or bones, including a fractured skull, compound fractures, broken jaw or ribs.
- Serious loss of blood, needing transfusion or lengthy treatment or incapacity.
- GBH includes the inflicting of serious psychiatric injury (subject to the evidence of an expert witness).

Manslaughter

Manslaughter is a charge that results from what is called a Partial Defence to the crime of Murder. Differing from a Complete Defence, as would be the case in showing self-defence, a Partial Defence means that the defendant is guilty of killing unlawfully, but that there are mitigating factors that make a charge of Murder inappropriate in the case.

Manslaughter is often charged where a person has thrown a punch that resulted in the death of another person. This charge will happen in these situations when it is clear in law that the intent to kill was not there in the throwing of that punch. This is so common an outcome that it has a name: **One Punch**

Manslaughter.

Attempted Murder

Attempted Murder is a tricky charge to prove as it requires the prosecution to successfully show that the accused committed an assault with intent to take life, rather than simply to cause GBH.

Murder

Murder is, of course, the unlawful taking of life.

Public Order Offences

There are various offences that fall under the Public Order Act (1986) and are sometimes chosen by police and prosecutors as charges alternative to those above. It is important to have a basic grasp of these offences, but especially the offence of Affray, which is a common charge brought against persons who have been seen acting violently in public.

Section 5

Used in less serious incidents of disorderly and anti-social behaviour, this charge applies to behaviour that is simply threatening or abusive, in any public or private place (not a dwelling), with intention or awareness that the behaviour may be disorderly, within the hearing or sight of a person likely to be caused **harassment, alarm**

or distress.

Example: You walk down a residential street shouting abusive language. This language is likely to cause harassment, alarm or distress to the residents of that street.

Section 4a

Section 4a is basically the same offence as 5, but is charged when the offender can be shown to have directly intended their actions to cause a person harassment, alarm or distress. In other words, when the disorderly behaviour is directed at someone, rather than just being general in an area.

For example, an offender is seen shouting, "Fuck you," **specifically to a person or persons.**

Section 4

Section 4 is the same as Section 4a, except that it involves a threatening or abusive words that are used with the intent that a person may fear that violence may be used against them. This is very similar to the offence of Assault.

For example, you walk down a residential street and see someone leaning out of a window. You shout, "Fuck off or I'll hurt you."

Section 3 — Affray

Affray is the public order offence that bears the greatest relevance to Rules of Engagement. This is because it can often be charged where several people are fighting in the street and it is impossible to determine which is at fault. It is very easy to fall into being charged with Affray, where there is insufficient evidence for investigators to determine whether you, or the people you fought with, are responsible for an incident of violence.

The definition of Affray is as follows:

Using or threatening unlawful violence toward any person in a way that might cause members of the public present at the scene to fear for their own safety.

An example of this is shown in the next scenario:

Scenario:

You walk down a street. A male appears in front of you and shouts an insult at you. You challenge him verbally. He steps closer. A fight breaks out between you and police subsequently arrive on scene. There are no witnesses or cameras, or if witnesses exist they are unable to state who is at fault, simply stating that a fight broke out and you and the male were fighting. Police could rightfully say that your behaviour could cause fear in members of the public, and seek a charge of Affray against both you and the male for your actions. Pleading self-defence in such a circumstance would be difficult, for reasons we will explore in detail later.

In summary, many situations where victims are drawn into a fight, rather than where they are obviously assaulted, can end up being dealt with as cases of Affray. Later, we will explore the concept of Life Vs Ego, and look at the threat of Affray in more detail.

Sections 2 and 1

Violent Disorder and Riot, respectively. These offences are outside the scope of this course, as they are not immediately relevant to the subject of self-defence.

Part 2 - The Definitions of Self-Defence Under UK Law

In the United Kingdom, the Crown Prosecution Service (CPS) lay out the foundation for self-defence with the following:

"The basic principles of self-defence are set out in (Palmer v R [1971] AC814) and approved in (R v McInnes, 55 Cr App R 551):

"It is both good law and good sense that a man who is attacked may defend himself. It is both good law and good sense that he may do, but only do, what is reasonably necessary.[3]"

In the 1971 case of Palmer v R, Lord Morris, presiding, added the following:

"If there has been an attack so that self-defence is reasonably necessary, it will be recognised that a person defending himself cannot weigh to a nicety the exact measure of his defensive action. If the jury thought that in a moment of unexpected anguish a person attacked had only done what he honestly and instinctively thought necessary, that would be the most potent evidence that only reasonable defensive action had been taken."

These statements are **legal precedents**. They have the power of law in this country. Yet, obviously, they contain subjective terms.

What, for example, does *reasonable* mean in the context of self-defence? Morris tells us that it is OK to use force to defend ourselves but we must only do what is reasonably necessary. But again, what is "reasonable"? Morris concedes that we cannot be expected to judge

3 Crown Prosecution Service guidance on self-defence (Violence Against the Person Incorporating the Charging Standard), UK Government Website (2018)

exactly what is reasonable in the heat of the moment, and states that we must only do what we instinctively believe, in the moment, to be necessary. Another abstract, without definition. What does "necessary" mean in this context?

The ambiguities around these statements are perhaps the source of many people's mistrust of self-defence law. It is possible, however, through investigation of case histories, and through a thorough understanding of police and prosecutor's procedures, to come to a more complete understanding of the law around self-defence, and to act with confidence when facing violence in your own life.

Understanding begins with good definitions. A good, and frequently quoted summation of the law is that any force used must be:

Reasonable
Proportionate
Necessary
In the circumstances as you believed them to be

To help us define these terms, consider this scenario:

Scenario:

You wake in the middle of the night. You hear smashing glass, and someone moving around downstairs. You open your bedroom door.

Torchlight plays on the walls in the stairwell and you find yourself less than a metre away from a male, who is dressed in black, his face covered with a balaclava and hood. He has a hammer in his hand. You immediately lash out, punching him hard in the jaw. He falls backwards, tumbling down the stairs, and lands at the bottom with one leg twisted unnaturally. He begins to scream in pain.

Reasonable Force

What is reasonable, in the eyes of the law? The simplest way of understanding this is to think of the conflict and subsequent investigation in terms of public perception and public interest. What if the above scenario happened and you found yourself in court facing the decision of 12 jurors who had to decide if your actions were correct? Would they find your actions reasonable? What if you showed the public a video of your actions?

Turns out, this is along the lines of how the law makes its judgement on reasonableness.

In a legal context, reasonable means that it is a decision or course of action a majority of ordinary people of 'reasonable firmness' would have taken if

they faced the same scenario as you.

In the case of your midnight intruder, isn't it likely that the overwhelming majority of people would agree that your actions were reasonable? Well then, so will the law. In the context of this scenario, it is very likely that the case would not reach court. An armed offender was in your house in the dead of night. So overwhelming would public opinion be that you were in the right that police or prosecutors would almost certainly decide not to pursue prosecution against you. Public interest is always considered when deciding whether or not to bring a prosecution.

Proportionate Force

Much easier to understand, proportionality is vital to staying lawful in your use of force. If the burglar has a hammer and you shove him away, your use of force falls way below the proportional level. You would have easily been proportional using a much greater degree of force in these circumstances, provided you honestly believed that the offender was going to use the hammer to attack you. Weapons are not the only thing that affects proportionality. It may be proportionate for you to pick up a weapon against an unarmed attacker if he has several co-offenders behind him. Or if he is twice your bodyweight. Or if you have a leg in a cast or are otherwise disabled.

Proportionality is about comparison. Police and prosecutors, and eventually magistrates, judges and juries, will weigh the threat you faced against the actions you took, to see if your actions matched, or were proportionate to, the threat. Proportionality involves the judicious application of common sense, and is inseparable from its brothers, reasonableness and necessity. It is reasonable and proportionate to push an armed burglar away because you see he has a weapon and think he is about to use it. It is not proportionate to stab an unarmed burglar multiple times with a kitchen knife, but it would be if the burglar also had a knife, or some other weapon, and was trying to use it on you.

Necessary Force

Necessity follows on from proportionality, but goes further. At the start of conflict, it must be asked, was the conflict itself necessary? There is no duty to retreat written into UK law (England and Wales — there is a duty to attempt retreat in Scotland, and in many states of the USA). However if you woke up and there was someone outside your locked home trying to break in, and you rushed outside and attacked them, you would find yourself on thin ice. Questions would be asked, such as why you didn't call police. Did you really need to go outside to attack them when you were inside, behind a locked door? If you went out the back and then around to the front to attack them, couldn't you have fled the scene to call police, instead of pursuing and attacking them? Force can of course be used to protect property, but such action will be judged far more harshly than force used to protect life. How much is a life worth, after all, compared to a window or a laptop?

After the initial defence, necessity again becomes relevant. You have punched a burglar, causing him to fall down the stairs. His legs are broken and he is writhing in pain and obviously unable to get up. You go downstairs and kick him repeatedly while he is on the floor. Is this force necessary to protect yourself? Clearly not. The initial push was necessary, and lawful, but this secondary use of force fails to meet the measure of necessity and is therefore,. unlawful. Consider also that it is now disproportionate. The broken offender lying at the bottom of your stairs now presents no threat to you; any use of force will probably be disproportionate to the threat you faced once he was incapacitated. Also, would the majority of people consider further attack against the burglar reasonable? (Putting aside of course a natural desire for retribution in cases of serious crime such as this.)

The Circumstances as You Believed Them to Be

Our final definition in this section deals with the concept of belief. The legal precedent quoted earlier in this section mentions that lawful self-defence means doing only what you believed was necessary to defend yourself or others. The concept of belief, then, is an important factor in legal terms.

Section 76 of the Criminal Justice and Immigration Act, 2008, adds to this concept by stating that your use of force in a violent situation will be legal if it is reasonable in the circumstances **as you reasonably believed them to be.**

This means, in simpler terms, that the precise facts of the situation are of secondary importance, in the eyes of the law, to your perception and interpretation of what happened and what you faced. But note the vital caveat:

Reasonably believed...

Here is the word reasonable again, and it means the same as it did before.

Consider the burglar on the stairs again. It is possible that he in no way intended to harm you with the hammer. But it certainly was reasonable for you, finding him on your stairs in the middle of the night, to believe that he was about to harm you.

Would the majority of ordinary people have

believed the same? Of course, and so this belief was reasonable. Your use of force will therefore be weighed against the threat of a man armed with a hammer, whether or not he later states he had no intention to use it to harm you.

Later, when we explore use of force justification, we will revisit the importance of stating your honest beliefs about the situation you faced.

Module 4 - The Two Thresholds to Violent Action

In Module 4, we will introducc you to Lawful Survival's framework for understanding and managing conflict escalation. We call this framework The Two Thresholds to Violent Action.

The Two Thresholds gives us the means to think about situations of escalating conflict in a measured and objective way, helping us not only to respond to conflict and threat in a tactically sound way, but also to correctly justify our responses after the fact.

By learning and applying the Two Threshold framework, you will have a solid foundation to your conflict management and use of force justifications.

Learning Outcomes:

- The Adrenal Threshold - What is the Adrenal Threshold?
- Why the Adrenal Threshold provides a

tactical justification to use force at a specific time.

- Why the Adrenal Threshold provides a legal justification to use force at a specific time.
- The Threat Threshold - Defining the moment in conflict where violent action becomes essential.
- The factors that affect where the Threat Threshold lies.

Part 1 - The Adrenal Threshold

In violent situations, fear is king. Most people, especially people without professional training, underestimate the effect fear has on people in violent situations.

Lawful Survival has conducted extensive research into the dynamics of violent incidents and the overwhelming effect of fear in deciding the results of those incidents. Though this is beyond the scope of Rules of Engagement, we will present you a summary of our findings here, as this will help you to understand the Threshold framework, and how it relates to Rules of Engagement and use of force justification.

- It is a person's capacity to control fear that most significantly decides what will happen if they are violently assaulted, not their level of training in combative techniques.
- The feelings of fear we feel in a violent or dangerous situation are collectively called the Acute

Stress Response, and adrenaline release is a part of that response

- Adrenal Freeze is what happens when a victim is overcome by their Acute Stress Response, and becomes paralysed, literally, with fear. In technical terms, a victim's higher cognitive processes — such as language processing and performance of complex movements — begin to shut down, causing an inability to reason, decide or act. This occurs often. In fact, in ordinary people who have no training and little or no experience of violence, total fear paralysis or Adrenal Freeze occurs in 88% of cases where such a person is violently assaulted.
- Freeze is devastating. Around 9 out of 10 cases where the victim freezes, the outcome is a total failure to mount an effective defence, resulting in injury or death.
- Not freezing is vital to success. 78% of incidents where the victim mounts a successful defence, they will not freeze.
- It is possible to come back from freeze and defend yourself, but only with extensive training and a little luck.
- **It is also possible to prevent freeze. This can be done one way only, by taking action.** The Acute Stress Response - and adrenaline - are designed to make you act. It is inaction that causes freeze. Even simple actions can prevent freeze, if taken consciously, and in time.

With these statistics in mind, let us move on to the Adrenal Threshold.

Scenario:

Imagine you are on a street late at night with a group of friends, making your way home after a night out. Two males turn on your group, threatening you and demanding that you fight with them. This comes completely out of the blue, a total shock to your system. You have gone from total relaxation to life-threatening conflict in a mere moment. You feel your adrenaline suddenly as an intense rush of fear, butterflies in the stomach, breathlessness, your thinking muddy, your mouth dry.

One of your group steps in the way of the aggressive males but they ignore her, jabbing a finger over her shoulder towards you, shouting abuse and threats. They want to hurt you. It is there in their words, in their actions, in the bared teeth, the wide, glaring eyes, the spittle coming out of their mouths as they shout at you. You think of wild dogs.

Your mind is shutting down. You cannot think.

The fear is so intense it takes over everything.

The distance is beginning to break down. If you do not act now, you never will.

You are at the Adrenal Threshold. The Acute Stress Response is fully engaged. Levels of stress hormones in your bloodstream are rising rapidly — adrenaline, cortisol — and causing the symptoms you can feel, such as dry mouth and shaking. This escalation of stress and fear is on a curve.

The curve leads to freeze.

If you do not act, you will freeze.

The Adrenal Threshold is the last moment in a conflict where you are still able to take action before fear overwhelms you and you freeze.

You will not reach the Adrenal Threshold in all situations. Sometimes you won't go near it. But it is essential that you are able to recognise when you are approaching it. **Cross the adrenal threshold without taking action and you will freeze. Take action before you reach the threshold and you will not freeze.**

Action does not always mean a use of force. Your action may be to run. It may even be to change your de-escalation tactic from talking and reasoning to aggressive, shouted warnings — "BACK AWAY". The one thing you must never do, from a tactical perspective, is take no action when you know you are approaching freeze. Taking no action means giving in to freeze. If you freeze, you will stand motionless as the attacker does whatever they want to do to you. Act, and you have a chance.

The Adrenal Threshold forms a small but significant part of a good use of force justification. If, during a violent incident, you felt yourself approaching freeze because you were so afraid, and that understanding pushed you into taking action, explaining this will be a powerful aspect to your justification for the use of force. Just consider these words as an example:

"He was getting closer and closer, shouting that he was going to kill me. I was more scared than I've ever been. I could feel my legs shaking and I couldn't speak any more. I couldn't think. I felt myself freezing in fear so I hit him as hard as I could to stop him hurting me."

Because of the definition of Assault in UK law, a victim's emotional state is a vital component of any use of force justification. If you were terrified, explain this. More of this later, when we look at building a good use of force justification.

Also note, that by the time you reach the Adrenal Threshold, you have also very likely crossed an evidential threshold whereby you are justified in the use of force because of the actions of the aggressor. For this reason, it is often — but not always — appropriate to resort to a pre-emptive use of force when you feel yourself reaching the Adrenal Threshold.

Part 2 - The Threat Threshold

Back to our scenario, but this time looking at it without the colouring of fear, and purely from a tactical viewpoint. We will this time see through the eyes of the female friend as she steps between the aggressive males and you, trying to protect you from harm.

Scenario:

You are faced with two males. Behind you is a male friend, the intended victim of the aggressive males. Your friend has already passed the Adrenal Threshold and is frozen and inactive. You continue to attempt de-escalation, but the males are becoming rapidly more aggressive. One of the males is pointing and shouting at both you and your friend behind you, threatening violence.

Based on what you already know about OODA and reactionary gaps, you know that at the distance the male is stood, he can initiate an attack at any moment and you will not have any realistic chance to defend yourself. You try to push the male backwards to create and maintain a gap, but he is simply too aggressive and keeps closing the space between you. At this moment you have already passed the Threat Threshold - the last moment or opportunity you have to take a pre-emptive action before entering the territory of terminal danger. Once you are past the Threat Threshold, whoever acts first will prevail, and whoever does not faces incapacitation and injury.

The Threat Threshold is the point in a conflict where, if you do not initiate violent action by way of pre-emptive striking, and instead the threat(s) initiates the violence, you risk incapacitation.

Another way of looking at the Threat Threshold is to think about how it is most often crossed. Of course, it is crossed when the threat initiates violent action by striking you, but we are talking about the time before that happens. In the overwhelming majority of cases, if the threat initiates violent action first, the victim will be incapacitated. Initiative matters in violent conflict.

Prior to the threat initiating violence, the Threat Threshold is most often crossed when it is no longer possible to maintain a reactionary gap.

Remember, pre-emptive striking is a component of

most successful uses of force in self-defence.

The Threat Threshold is a vital piece of strategic understanding, and should be a part of any training regime. There are no hard and fast rules that will define where the Threat Threshold is in every situation. It is subjective to the individual. Therefore you must be trained experientially to recognise it, and be able to verbally justify why you believe it has been reached.

It is impossible to adequately justify pre-emptive force without being able to understand and state why there was no other reasonable option — in other words, why the Threat Threshold had been reached.

In general, tactical justification *is* legal justification. If, for example, your tactical reason for pre-emptively striking a male was that his hand was going rapidly for a pocket and you believed he was going for a weapon, that is also your legal justification for your subsequent use of force. Every situation will be different. What is constant is that you must adapt and make that split second decision to use force before force can be used decisively against you.

Part 3 - Factors Affecting the Threat Threshold

There are many factors that affect where the Threat Threshold is in any given situation. It is never possible to generalise. Certain things will cause the Threat Threshold to occur sooner, and certain things later. Here are some examples of factors that will affect where the Threat Threshold is in a violent incident.

- Size of attacker vs size of victim. Quite clearly, if the threat is twice the size and weight of the victim, the victim's Threat Threshold arrives much earlier in the situation than if the sizes were more closely matched. In simpler terms, the smaller victim cannot afford to take chances; if the larger attacker gets hold of the victim, the assault is pretty much already over.
- Note that comparisons of all sorts are some of the most critical elements of any use of force justification. Size, age, disability — even equipment or dress can be relevant comparisons.
- Numbers for and against. Obviously the Threat Threshold arrives earlier if you are outnumbered many to one.
- Weapons. The presence or suggestion of a weapon raises risk and threat level, lowering the Threat Threshold (making it occur sooner).
- Behaviour and level of aggression. A highly irrational and aggressive threat obviously lowers the threat threshold.
- Signs of advanced acute stress response (adrenalisation) in the threat. Signs of adrenalisation, such as bulging eyes, deterioration of language to

single syllable grunts, or puffing out the chest, signify that the threat is at or approaching the peak of their escalation curve and will likely attack at any moment. If you can articulate what you saw clearly, such signs build a solid justification for the pre-emptive use of force.

- Skill and experience. If you have no training whatsoever, you may state that. If the threat takes a stance that looks skilled, you may state that too. This is another comparison.
- Location and environment. If you are in a remote location, this will raise the stakes as you are further from help. If you are in a dangerous location, such as on the hard shoulder of a motorway, this also lowers the Threat Threshold, justifying force earlier in the curve.

Summary:

Good decision making and subsequent use of force justification relies on you being able to explain where the Threat Threshold is in any situation, and why you believed it had been reached when you took action.

Module 5 - Life v Ego - The Morality of Self-Defence

In this module, we will take our first steps in understanding how the law is applied to real-world situations and, more importantly, we will explore the vital difference between using force in legitimate self-defence — that is, defence of life — and using force to defend ego. We will also revisit the criminal offence of Affray and explain why Affray is often the charging result where someone has used force to defend their ego, and not their life.

Learning Outcomes:

- Beginning to apply the law — this is the first module in which we will explore how the law is applied to real-world situations. You will learn why necessity is a vital component of justifying force, and why necessity usually equates to a defence of life, whereas a lack of necessity usually equates to a defence of ego.

- You should, by the end of this module, understand what duty to retreat means, and how it applies to self-defence situations.
- We explore what a typical defence of ego looks like.
- We discuss why affray is a likely outcome in cases where someone has used force to defend ego.

Part 1 - Beginning to Apply the Law - Necessity and the Defence of Life

Let us revisit what the law says about self-defence.

"It is both good law and good sense that a man who is attacked may defend himself. It is both good law and good sense that he may do, but only do, what is reasonably necessary."

Palmer v R [1971]

This piece of case law is the very foundation of lawful self-defence in the UK. Let us think in a little more detail about what it says.

- A person should be able to defend themselves **if attacked**.
- They should be able to do only what is **necessary** to defend themselves.

These simple statements seem easy to understand

and apply. Indeed, where there is a clear assault — where one person clearly attacks another — they are as simple as they sound.

Scenario:

> *You are outside a building talking with a friend. A male — Attacker 1 — comes out of the building and for some reason approaches you rapidly and aggressively. When he reaches you, he reaches out his right hand and pushes you backwards, violently. It is all you can do to keep your balance and avoid falling. You see another male join Attacker 1. We will call this male Attacker 2.*

At this point, is it fair to say you have been assaulted?

In any self-defence situation, there is a large degree of subjectivity. However, in this situation, it is reasonable for you to believe you have been assaulted, and that further harm is about to be visited upon you.

Let us first consider a duty to retreat. Again, there is no requirement for you to attempt to escape before resorting to use of force in UK law as it applies to England and Wales. The law in Scotland varies in this regard in that it requires you to attempt escape prior to using force, and to only use force if escape is impossible or fails. Regardless of the difference in jurisdictional approach, you should always have a justification ready to justify why you did not attempt to escape. Even in England and Wales, where this justification is not legally required, it will strengthen your explanation that force was your only recourse.

In this situation, is escape an option?

We would argue it is not, due to the immediate nature of the threat. Is it reasonable that you can turn and run now? Or is it reasonable to believe that were you to attempt this, you would raise the risk of harm to yourself close to certainty?

In this case, there is a very strong case for use of force, and a very strong argument against attempting to retreat, whatever jurisdiction you find yourself in.

Secondly, let's consider the assault. It is reasonable to state that you have been assaulted. A common assault has already occurred not because of the shove, but because of the implication of the shove — words or actions that have caused you to apprehend immediate, unlawful violence.

Remember the test of Reasonable that we defined in Module 3? It applies here. At this point, if we showed 100 ordinary people a video of this scenario and asked them if they thought you were about to be attacked and harmed, the majority would certainly agree yes, you were about to be the victim of unlawful and immediate violence.

In other words, an assault has occurred and there is already a justification for use of force in self-defence.

Any action taken now will be a defence of life, and not a defence of ego.

Part 2 - In Defence of Ego

Now let us consider defence of ego, as opposed to defence of life. Consider the all too common scenario:

Scenario:

> *You are walking along and bump into Male 2, who is waiting at the side of a road. Male 2 becomes aggressive, splaying his arms out and becoming verbally abusive. Male 2 says to you words to the effect of, "You want some? You want a fucking problem?"*

Unlike our previous scenario, in this case there is no initial attack by Male 2, just an aggressive approach and an invitation to fight. At this point in the proceedings, if you pre-emptively strike Male 2, is that a reasonable use of force? Is it necessary? If you are in a duty to retreat jurisdiction, have you demonstrated a reasonable attempt to retreat from the situation without force?

There are some situations where yes, it would be

necessary for you to use pre-emptive force against Male 2. Factors such as size, numbers, the nature of the threats, will all come into play here. However, and this is the important point, **where a challenge to fight is laid down, it is not a definite conclusion that violence will follow if you respond by creating distance and backing down**. There is an unwritten expectation implicit to the law that expects you to make some attempt to de-escalate such conflict before using force. Once again, even if you live in England and Wales, where there is no explicit duty to retreat, the law will want to see an effort to avoid conflict in situations such as this.

There are clearly situations where force is necessary even at the point of verbal threat. The point to remember here is that, in this specific situation, there is significant doubt as to whether force is necessary here, at the verbal stage. **The more effort you make to de-escalate before using force, the safer your legal position will be. In cases of social violence where a challenge is laid down, there is usually a point where de-escalation — either verbal or by walking away — can prevent the situation from becoming violent. If you take the opportunity to de-escalate and your attempt fails, you will have at least built evidence of your unwillingness to engage in violence, demonstrating that you are the victim in this situation.**

Consider that a single punch can readily kill someone, even if that is not your intention. Facing such a threat, is it worth risking the death of another human being simply because they challenged you to fight, and were verbally abusive? Is there not a moral duty, even if not written into law, to attempt to de-escalate — to retreat — from such a situation? **Are you not acting in defence of ego if you strike first and injure or kill the aggressor in front of you?**

These are questions a court may well ask you if you go ahead and use force in such a situation. Know this for certain: **use of pre-emptive force in such a situation will not be easy or straightforward to justify.**

Scenario:

Imagine viewing the following incident on CCTV, with no audio, and then having to make a rational decision about who was at fault.

> *Male 1 stops in front of Male 2. There is a verbal exchange, which you cannot hear. Male 1 then removes his coat, revealing an orange shirt, and throws it onto the ground between Male 2 and himself. Male 2 appears to bounce on his feet, as if limbering up for a fight. Stopping the video there,*

consider this: From the perspective of an outside observer, who is the aggressor in this situation?

The difficulty any reasonable person would have answering that question, with only this remote viewpoint to go on, creates a problem if one of the parties later decides to offer a legal defence of self-defence to any criminal charge.

This scenario appears to be an example of where one party has challenged another party to a fight, or has provoked the other party by way of abuse or threatening words or behaviour, and where the target party has risen to the bait and chosen to engage in violence.

If this scenario becomes violent, who will be at fault? Clearly, both parties will claim innocence and state that the other party caused the issue. If the only evidence to decide the case is this footage, how will Police, and the Courts decide what outcome is just?

This is the primary danger of acting in defence of ego: all too often, because you are acting without morality, you will leave behind you no compelling evidence of right action, and it will be very difficult for you to plead self-defence to any subsequent criminal charge.

Finally, remember this: In cases of social violence

where a challenge is laid down, there is usually a point where de-escalation — either verbal or by walking away — can prevent the situation from becoming violent. If you take the opportunity to de-escalate and your attempt fails, you will have at least built evidence of your unwillingness to engage in violence, demonstrating that you are the victim in this situation.

Part 3 - The Charge of Affray

Affray is a charge that commonly results from a scenario where one person is aggressive towards another and the 'victim' rises to the bait and responds in kind, defending ego rather than defending life.

As stated by the Crown Prosecution Service, the charging standard for Affray requires that:

Under section 3 of the Act, it must be proved that a person has used or threatened:

- unlawful violence;
- towards another;
- and his conduct is such as would cause;
- a person of reasonable firmness;
- present at the scene;
- to fear for his personal safety.

In simple terms, Affray is a charge that can be levelled against participants of violent incidents where their behaviour would cause any reasonable person at the scene to fear for their safety. Often, where Police attend a scene where two people are or have been fighting, and it is unclear who is the attacker as both are as aggressive as each other, a charge of Affray will be sought against both participants and will often be authorised by prosecutors.

Affray then, is a very real possibility in any situation where someone acts to preserve ego, and not to preserve life. In cases where two people agree to fight and then proceed to fight, Affray is extremely likely. You cannot claim to have acted in self-defence in your violence against another person if you first agreed to fight with that person.

In professional circles, a conflict where two people agree to fight, and then fight, is called a Match Fight. The vast majority of such situations in public will be found to be unlawful, with both participants facing the potential for criminal charges after the fact. This is because, fundamentally, the violence that happens in such situations is in defence of ego, and not in defence of life.

Module 6 - Tactical vs legal - The Rule of Balance in Use of Force Justification

In this module, we will introduce you to Lawful Survival's Rule of Balance, a proven framework for making force decisions under the life and death pressure of a violent situation. By understanding the Rule of Balance, you will build a fluid understanding of how the law relates to violent situations in the real world, and how you can practically and dynamically assess where you are in any situation in relation to the law, and the tactics you must use to guarantee survival.

Learning Outcomes:

- The Rule of Balance — We explain the Rule of Balance, and why it is an essential tool for navigating the dangerous waters of violent assault.
- The Tactical Imperative — What is the

Tactical Imperative?

- The Legal Imperative — What is the Legal Imperative?
- Earlier vs Later - How timing relates to the Rule of Balance, and helps you to remain lawful.
- The Knife Edge between the Balance - what it is and what it means to you and your survival. How can you widen the margins and increase your chances of safety?

Part 1 - The Rule of Balance

Not all self-defence situations are the same. To begin, we will model the real world by simplifying violent incidents into three main categories.

Category A - Blitz Attack

Some situations begin with the **victim unaware of the threat**, and subject to a sudden and unexpected violent assault. We call such situations Ambush or Blitz attacks. In such situations, using force in **self-defence is easy to justify legally**, as the **attacker has initiated the attack** and the victim is responding — defending against that attack. The problem, of course, is that real life is not like the movies, and the **victim is HIGHLY likely to be incapacitated** before they can take action.

Category B - Aware Victim

The second type of scenario is where the **victim is aware of the threat** before it becomes physically violent, **but takes no action** and is then attacked by the aggressor. This leads to a scenario similar to Category A, where the attacker makes the first move — hits first — and the victim then attempts to use force to defend themselves. Again, this is **easy to defend legally** as the victim did not initiate the physical component of the incident. However, just as in Category A, the **victim is HIGHLY likely to be incapacitated** before they can mount any kind of effective defence.

Category C - Aware Victim / Pre-emptive Attack

The third, and least common, category of violent incident is one where the **victim is aware of the threat** before it becomes physically violent, **and takes pre-emptive action to stop the threat** — usually by launching their own blitz attack on the suspected aggressor(s). This scenario is the only one where the **victim can enjoy a high probability of survival**, but is the **hardest to justify legally**, as it is the victim that launches the attack.

Can you see the conflict in every situation between needing to remain safe physically, and needing to remain safe legally?

With this conflict in mind, let us remind ourselves of some core tactical and legal principles:

- If an aggressor is within striking range and they strike first, you will not be able to reliably stop that attack. If it is effective, you will be incapacitated. This means pre-emptive use of force represents the only viable, reliable, tactical option for surviving violent conflict.
- Pre-emptive use of force is permissible in UK law, provided that it is reasonable, and necessary in the circumstances as the victim believed them to be.

Looking at these principles, the conflict between physical safety and legal safety becomes more obvious.

Now let us introduce the Rule of Balance:

In every second of a violent incident, and in every action, there is a Tactical Imperative and a Legal Imperative. They are opposites, and do not easily co-exist. Increase one, and you decrease the other. Where you are safest legally, you are in the most danger tactically. Where you are safest tactically, you are in the most danger legally. In the middle of these poles is a knife edge, which you must learn to walk if you are to survive violent incidents intact, both physically and legally.

In simpler terms, in every second of an incident, you must observe what is happening, and you must decide what to do about what you see and hear. This decision will be based on your tactical understanding, and your legal understanding, and it will be affected by your conflicting needs not to be harmed and not to go to prison or face other legal consequences.

Let us continue by breaking down the conflicting Imperatives.

Tactical Imperative

The Tactical Imperative is the absolute necessity to take the right actions to allow you to prevail in the physical aspect of the incident. It is an imperative to read the threat correctly, second by second, and act to keep yourself and others safe, and to stay on top of the situation.

The Tactical Imperative is the ongoing need to take only those actions that will keep you safe from physical harm and avoid any action that could result in the threat gaining the upper hand and harming you or other innocent parties present at the scene.

Legal Imperative

The Legal Imperative is the absolute necessity to take only those actions that will keep you safe from legal consequences, and to avoid any action that could result in you facing legal consequences after the fact.

To aid in your understanding of these Imperatives, and their application, it is helpful to think about what would happen if we followed these Imperatives to the extreme. Remember the rule: Increase one and you decrease the other. At the extremes, only one imperative can exist.

Revisit our categories. What happened in Category A? The victim was ambushed and assaulted. They took no action in their own defence. Which Imperative have they respected, and which have they ignored?

In Category A, the victim took no action. They were incapacitated by violent assault. Tactically, this was the worst possible course of action and the worst possible outcome. The **Tactical Imperative** was ignored. Legally, this is the best possible outcome. They will face no legal action, should they survive, as they took no action in their own defence. No justification is even required. The **Legal Imperative** has been fully respected.

In Category C, the victim takes pre-emptive action. This is the best Tactical option as it is the only one that provides a good chance of physical safety against an aggressive attacker offering the threat of violence. By striking pre-emptively and incapacitating the threat, the victim is respecting the **Tactical Imperative**. However, by striking before the aggressor, the victim enters more dangerous ground legally, and moves away from the **Legal Imperative**. A good justification is going to be required for the victim to survive legally.

We can take this to an imagined extreme, to further demonstrate the Rule of Balance.

Imagine Category D: The 'victim' is at a bar and sees a male who appears to be speaking aggressively to another male. Shortly after, the aggressive male comes over to the bar, near to where the 'victim' is. Suspecting that the male might become aggressive to him, the 'victim' takes pre-emptive action and punches the male hard in the jaw, incapacitating him.

In this imagined scenario, Tactical safety is guaranteed — the suspect male has been incapacitated before even having the chance to threaten the 'victim'. But obviously, this is morally and legally inexcusable. The 'victim' isn't even a victim in this case, but is instead an attacker. He has assaulted this other male without any legal grounds. In this extreme case, the

Tactical Imperative has been respected in the extreme, and the **Legal Imperative** ignored in the extreme.

Part 2 - Earlier vs Later

Lastly, it is important to understand that, in general, **following the Tactical Imperative means using force earlier in a situation, whereas following the Legal Imperative means using force later.**

Later = Safer legally and more dangerous tactically.

Earlier = Safer tactically and more dangerous legally.

Why is this the case? Being able to answer this question is the key to understanding self-defence law.

You are tactically safer using force earlier because the earlier you use force in the incident — and in the escalation curve — the more likely you are to gain surprise and capture the initiative. **You are legally less safe if you use force earlier** because there will have been less opportunities to build a lawful justification for use of force before you actually used force.

You are legally safer using force later because the later you use force in the incident — and in the escalation curve — the more likely you are to have built a lawful justification for use of force before you actually used force. **You are tactically less safe if you use force later** because the later you use force the more time the threat(s) has to set up a blitz attack, and the more time they have to overcome their own fear and take action. If you allow them pre-emptive action, for example, you are almost guaranteed to be overwhelmed and incapacitated.

Part 3 - The Knife-Edge

The extremes of the Imperatives exist as a thought experiment; obviously it is not a rational answer to attack so early as to be the aggressor, or to take no action and allow yourself to be assaulted. We have an overall imperative — a Moral Imperative, if you will — to find the balance between Tactical and Legal Imperatives. This is never easy. It may even be impossible to find the perfect balance, because one factor will always decrease as the other increases.

What this means in practice is that we must, in following either imperative, accept a measure of risk. You cannot walk a knife-edge in real life. You must widen the parameters to make passage possible. Widening in either direction means risk in the other. How much risk we accept on either side is up to the individual, and will depend on your own opinions, morality, and the role you are in when you come up against a violent incident.

Most civilians, for example, who are trained in self-defence, if they do not freeze, will tend towards the Tactical Imperative. They will try to take action to strike and damage the threat, and will not, in the moment, spare much consideration to the legal consequences of their actions.

Most untrained people, if they do not freeze, will tend towards the Legal Imperative, albeit subconsciously. They will hesitate and worry about hurting another person for long enough that the threat can incapacitate them — thereby ignoring the Tactical Imperative, or simply being unaware that it exists.

Any professional in a role that is exposed to violence must tolerate greater extremes of risk — by denying the tactical in favour of the legal — due to the often unfairly imposed judgements they face at the end of any use of force. Consider the following examples, presented to aid in understanding various role approaches to violence.

If faced with violent assault, how would an A&E doctor respond? Where would this be in relation to the Imperatives? [Faced with no backup from NHS, and no training, if they don't freeze, the doctor will still take no action, obeying the legal imperative to the extreme, preferring injury to any risk to career.]

And an armed police officer? [Faced with a genuine threat to life, the armed police officer will always obey the Tactical Imperative, but will not do so to extremes. There will always be time given to build a justification for any use of force, where that time is available. Where it is not available, for example in the case of a sudden weapon threat, lethal force will be used in following the Tactical Imperative.]

How about a teacher, faced with an out of control student threatening violence? [Similar to the NHS staff, a teacher is likely to follow the legal imperative, and disregard the tactical imperatives, putting themselves at risk. This is as much a product of the absence of training as it is any moral decision.]

Or a door supervisor who is facing an aggressive and threatening male outside a busy door? [Many staff tend towards the Tactical Imperative, at the expense of the Legal Imperative. This is understandable as they face frequent and serious threat with a minimum of training, however it does result in frequent prosecutions against door staff in the UK.]

Conclusion:

In conclusion, the Rule of Balance means that, in any situation where we face threat of violence from other people, effective self-defence means finding a middle ground between Tactical and Legal imperatives. In the next module, we'll look at how you can widen the knife-edge between Tactical and Legal, and give yourself the best chance of coming out of any situation both legally and physically intact.

Module 7 - Building a Lawful Justification for Use of Force (Before and During Conflict)

This module brings us at last into the realm of the practical, and is the most important of all the modules in this book.

In Module 7, we will introduce you to the most fundamental concept in lawful self-protection. Most writing on the subject of self-defence law deals with the act of violence, but the truth is that the most important moments of a violent incident are the moments before the conflict becomes physical. It is here, in the preliminary seconds, that you can begin to build an unshakeable legal and moral foundation to your actions, laying down evidence of right action that will carry you through even the worst of situations.

Module 7 is the backbone of Rules of Engagement, and is the backbone for your understanding of lawful self-defence. By grasping the principles in this module, you can learn how to widen the knife-edge between the Tactical Imperative and the Legal Imperative, forging a path that is wide enough to carry you home to safety.

Learning Outcomes:

- Widening the knife-edge. How we can respect both the Tactical and Legal Imperatives.
- Thinking like an Investigator - How investigators approach the aftermath of a violent incident. How understanding the logical process of investigation helps you to navigate the turbulent legal waters and build evidence that will contribute to a good use of force justification.
- The 100 Yard Witness. How we can indirectly communicate our intentions and motives to anyone present at a scene, including CCTV cameras.
- The scales of blame. How even small gestures, words and actions can tip these delicate scales one way or the other, influencing the investigative and judicial decisions of those who stand in judgement of you.

Part 1 - Widening the Knife-Edge

In module 6, we introduced you to the Rule of Balance, and the two opposites, the Tactical and Legal Imperatives. We said that, to survive physically and legally intact, you have to walk the knife-edge between these two imperatives.

In reality, we cannot do this without widening the path. We need a way to increase our opportunities, both in terms of satisfying the Legal Imperative and the Tactical Imperative.

Here is perhaps the most important understanding about self-defence law that we can tell you:

The foundations for a legal defence are laid before a violent incident even becomes physical, and are built upon with every action taken during the physical stage of the conflict.

Let us consider what this means.

Most people, if they are able to fight back against a violent attacker, will not consider the legal situation until after the conflict has been resolved. They then try to answer the Legal Imperative by telling police what happened, and stating that they did not cause it.

But what do you think the attacker will tell police? It is an unfortunate fact that most violent offenders know the law and how to lie to police far better than most victims. It is a necessary part of their way of life. A hazard of the trade. They have a lot of practise.

What if we didn't wait until it was over to start thinking about the law?

To understand this, let us take a step back and consider a violent incident from the point of view of a police officer, who has been called to attend a violent incident.

Part 2 - Thinking Like an Investigator

First, consider the following scenario.

Scenario:

You're a male approaching a club you like to drink in. You're with your partner, in this case a female. At the door are two men you assume to be door staff, although they are casually dressed. As you reach the rope line, one of them says, "You're not coming in here." The other laughs and says, "You look like a cunt". Now they're both laughing and your significant other is tugging on your arm trying to take you away from the situation. You don't move; fear is already starting to take hold of you.

"The fuck you going to do about it, Cunt?" says the one on the right, coming forward and standing well within your personal space.

You put your hands up and offer an apology, and then turn to leave. As you walk away, one of the males rushes and grabs you, pulling you back into the conflict.

"Said what you gonna do, Cunt?"

You know that he is going to hit you. You see his fist clench. You tip towards the Tactical Imperative and punch him in the throat before he can hit you. Then, before he falls, you knee him hard in the groin. Down he goes, incapacitated. The other male runs at you and misses with a wild punch. You get in a couple of strikes and knock him out. He falls, bleeding heavily from the face.

At that moment, a police car rounds the corner. Its roof lights up, throwing blinding blue strobe light up the surrounding walls. A police officer gets out and runs towards you.

In this scenario, two males have behaved aggressively towards you. You have tried to leave the situation, but one of the males has grabbed you, issuing a further challenge. You act pre-emptively and incapacitate both males. The police then attend.

Take a moment now, with the scenario fresh in your mind, and decide if your actions were lawful.

Now, what do the police see? The answer may seem obvious, but most people do not catch all the details.

First, the police see a male — you — stood over two incapacitated males. You are an immediate threat to the police. Remember, they do not know you. They have never met you, and they we're not there when the conflict happened. Let us assume you comply with their orders immediately and without hesitation. It is likely they will arrest you and remove you from the scene. You will later be questioned — we will speak more about this in Modules 8 and 9. They will then investigate the incident to determine what happened and who was at fault.

How will they investigate?

Obviously, they will need a way to rebuild the incident so they can see what happened. This means, in practice, finding independent witnesses (IW). An IW is a witness without a personal connection to those involved. Because of their lack of connection to the involved parties, their testimony of the incident is considered the most reliable. (The best IW is of course CCTV.)

This leads us on to the next concept, the 100 yard witness.

Part 3 - The 100 Yard Witness

Imagine, in the context of the scenario described in the previous section, that the only IW to this incident is an 80 year old male who was walking his dog when the incident occurred. He was about 100 yards away when he heard some shouting. He does not hear too well, nor see too well. What will he tell police? Take a moment to consider what you think he will say when questioned, based on the description of the scenario you were given in the previous section. And bear in mind, his testimony is the most important piece of information — and evidence — available to the investigating officer.

Here is an example of an account that could be given by this elderly gentleman.

> *I was out with the dog — she needs to walk just before bed — and I saw a couple right over there walking towards that building. When they were about ten metres away from it I saw another man come up to the couple. The woman seemed to try to pull the first man away but he wouldn't go. He put his hands up — I don't know why — and then he turned to go but the second man grabbed him. I*

didn't hear anything said but I think they were talking. Then the first man hit the second man several times in the face and head and the second man fell over. A third man then ran up and the first man hit that man too, also knocking him down. Then the first man and the woman walked away.

Can you see the problem? If you read this statement carefully, it is hard to see who is at fault. The roles of victim and offender are not clearly defined. The old man's account does not absolve you; it merely states that someone came up to you and you hit them, and also hit another male, knocking both down. You know the truth, of course, but the police officer does not. Neither does the Police Sergeant, nor the Crown Prosecutor who will read the charge file and make a decision about whether or not it is in the public interest to pursue a prosecution against you for two counts of assault. This is the inherent problem with relying on witnesses; they may not see or hear everything and may not report correctly what occurred.

Part 4 - The Scales of Blame

Whenever you think about the law and self-defence, always have in your mind a set of scales. On the one side are placed all the details available to investigators that point to you being an innocent victim of a violent incident, using lawful self-defence to protect yourself from harm. On the other are all the details available to investigators that point to you being as guilty or more guilty of a violent offence as the person or persons who confronted you.

Let us revisit the 100 Yard Witness's account once more with this set of scales in mind. What did the man tell police in his account?

In your favour:

- You turned to go early in the conflict, but were stopped by one of the males.
- You put your hands up. If the elderly male saw this as a defensive gesture, and told police as much, this goes in your favour.
- You only hit the first male after he grabbed you.

Against you:

- You hit two males.
- You threw the first punch.
- Your significant other tried to pull you away but you would not go with her.
- Neither of the males hit you, though one tried after you incapacitated the first, and you are uninjured.

Try to see this situation from the point of view of an investigator. To do that you have to be a detached observer. This incident, from the point of view of the IW, does not look good for you. All the police can do is gather the closest approximation of the facts from whatever witnesses and cameras there are at the scene. In this case, you have made no effort to control the incident and leave evidence of the lawful intent behind your actions, and you have made no effort to demonstrate to witnesses that you are an innocent party. You have left the situation to chance, and in this case chance, and the witness, have not helped your cause. Remember that the police were not there when this incident happened. Only the old man was. His third hand report is now all that your future hangs on. It is not a good situation.

But if we could do the incident over again, how could we change the outcome? One way is of course to abandon the Tactical Imperative and take no action in your own self-defence. You would be beaten to the floor. If you then survived, and your partner survived, you would have no legal case to answer. You would be a victim.

Clearly this is not a viable option.

What else could we do? How could we act before, during and after the incident to change any witness statements for the better?

Building Evidence to Tip the Scales

The answer to our dilemma lies in trying to answer the Legal Imperative early in the situation. In the case of a blitz attack, of course, none of this applies; you are thrown straight into violence and must fight for your life, but then the evidence would likely show a blitz attack and provide you a more robust defence for use of force.

In this situation, however, there was ample opportunity to take action to build evidence before the use of force. Many socially violent encounters, along with offering the opportunity and potential necessity for pre-emptive use of force, offer the chance to build evidence before the violence starts, and you must take full advantage of such an opportunity.

Consider the following revised situation:

You're a male approaching a club you like to drink in. You're with your partner, in this case a female. At the door are two men you assume to be door staff, although they are casually dressed. As you reach the rope line, one of them says, "You're not coming in here." The other laughs and says, "You look like a cunt. " Now they're both laughing and your significant other is tugging on your arm trying to take you away from the situation. You go with her, but walking sideways so you can see the males.

"The fuck you going to do about it, Cunt?" says the one on the right, coming forward and standing well within your personal space.

You put your hands up and offer an apology, and then turn to leave. As you walk away, one of the males rushes and grabs you, pulling you back into the conflict.

"Said what you gonna do, Cunt?"

You know that he is going to hit you. You see his fist clench. You tip towards the Tactical Imperative but also consider the Legal Imperative. You raise your hands in a defensive manner, palms out as if to say, "Stop!". You shout, "BACK AWAY! BACK AWAY!" The male closes the distance and you shove him backwards, continuing to shout your warnings.

Your shove creates distance but again he closes. His fist is still clenched. You now completely obey the Tactical Imperative and punch him in the throat before he can hit you. Then, before he falls, you knee him hard in the groin. Down he goes, incapacitated. The other male runs at you and you manage to shout, "BACK AWAY!" again before he misses with a wild punch. You get in a couple of strikes and knock him out. He falls, bleeding heavily from the face.

At that moment, a police car rounds the corner. Its roof lights up, throwing blinding blue strobe light up the surrounding walls. A police officer gets out and runs towards you. She is shouting, as is your partner, but you can't hear either of them because your Acute Stress Response is causing auditory exclusion.

What changes have we made to the victim's behaviours? And what will the independent witness now say about what he saw?

I was out with the dog — she needs to walk just before bed — and I saw a couple right over there walking towards that building. When they were about ten metres away from it I saw another man come up to the couple. The woman seemed to try to pull the first man away and he went with her a few paces but the other man went after him. The first man put his hands up — I think it was defensive because I heard him shout, "BACK AWAY!" and then he turned to go but the second man grabbed him. The first man shouted, "BACK AWAY!" again and pushed the second man away, but the second man was being very aggressive and went back towards the first man. The first man then hit the second man and knocked him down. The third man then ran at the first man and again the first man shouted, "Back away," but the third man ignored this warning and tried to hit the first man. The first man hit him then and knocked him down too. Then the police arrived.

Take some time now to consider this revised statement and make a note of the details that will go on our scales of blame.

In your favour:

- You turned to go at the start of the incident, showing a willingness to walk away.

- You put up your hands in a defensive manner, showing you were not the aggressor.
- You shouted, "BACK AWAY!" at both males, warning them to leave you alone and signifying that you did not want the violent confrontation that was being offered.
- You again turned and tried to leave but were grabbed.
- You pushed the male away, trying again to end the situation without violence.
- The male came towards you again, aggressively, which is when you used force. There is no doubt that the male, not you, was the instigator of this violent confrontation.

Against you:

- You hit two males who did not hit you, though one tried to hit you.

There is now an excellent chance that the right and fair decisions will be made by police in this circumstance. The IW has raised several points that will sit on your side of the scale, and only one that sits against you. Even that last need not necessarily end up counting against you, as it is simply an action you took that can be explained by the points already raised. Yes you hit the males, but you did so because they were a threat to you and your partner.

In summary, then, in this situation there were

several things you did that improved your chances of a good legal outcome, before and during the conflict. In other words, you attended to the Legal Imperative before the violence even started, leaving you free and ready to attend to the Tactical Imperative when it mattered the most.

In simple terms, you left evidence in your wake for the witnesses and cameras to see and the investigators to follow, evidence that tipped the scales in your favour.

This is a process that you should strive to achieve in any violent or potentially violent situation. In some situations it will be easier than others. In the case of a blitz attack, where you have no warning and are thrown into violence, there is no opportunity to take pre-emptive action to build evidence. However, even in the case of a blitz attack, if you overcome the first attacker, there are often opportunities to inject evidence by attempting de-escalation of secondary threats. In other words, you knock down the first threat and then shout a warning at the second threat before engaging.

No matter the difficulty, these principals of evidence-building apply to every situation. In any Use of Force Justification, tiny things matter. A gesture, a simple word overheard, can be enough to send the scale irrevocably one way or the other. Take nothing for granted. Leave nothing to chance. The consequences of failure are life-changing.

To finish this module, consider other words and

actions that might tip the scales in your favour in any incident. Also consider ideas of words or actions that might tip the scales against you.

Here are some examples:

- **Walking away**. This means any attempt by you to move away from the threats. It includes a change in direction that force a threat to either break off their aggressive approach or change direction to follow you. Obviously, if they follow you, you have excellent evidence that they gave you no choice but to defend yourself. It builds a pattern of behaviour for both you and the threats. Each movement, change of direction, crossing the street, entering or leaving a building, counts as one piece of evidence to put on the scales — if there is a witness or camera to see it.
- **Use of loud dialogue in de-escalation and warning**. Shouting things such as, "GET BACK!" or, "ABACK AWAY!" are a quintessential part of Use of Force Justification. They cause witnesses to look in your direction. They say clearly that you do not want the distance closed, that you do not want to fight. When they are ignored, they build a pattern of behaviour that paints the threat in a very bad light. It is also important to note that you being in fear of violence is an essential component of your claiming that your use of force was self-defence. Shouting at someone to leave you alone suggests this fear. It is

therefore essential practice, and weighty evidence to tip the scale. Every warning counts as a new piece of evidence in your favour.

- **Body language**. Holding one or both of your hands out, palm out, fingers spread. It's like you're trying to stop a car — in fact, police call one hand held up and out the Number One Stop Sign. This gesture and posture means stop in every language, and if you are saying stop, how can anyone argue that you wanted or initiated the violence that follows? Body language such as this defensive posture should be cultured so that it does not look like a martial arts stance but like an ordinary person asking another person to stop. It should be exaggerated and large so that witnesses even 100 yards away can see it and interpret it clearly. Every use of such a gesture counts as a piece of evidence that weighs down the scale in your favour.

- **Pushing away**. If all else fails and the threat(s) get too close, pushing away serves as an interim measure, a lower use of force designed to give the threat(s) another chance to do the right thing. This can be backed up with loud, verbal warnings. Every such movement and warning is more evidence in your favour.

- **Stopping any use of force at the earliest opportunity**. If you do use force against a threat, and that threat becomes incapacitated, you must not continue to use force against that threat unless there is a very good reason to do so. Once a threat falls, it is very likely that the 'necessary' criterion for a lawful use of force is no longer met. Remember that Reasonable, Proportionate and Necessary are **ongoing criteria**. I have seen situations that have resulted in charges against a victim of an assault because their use of force, necessary and lawful in the beginning, did not stop early enough and crossed the line into unnecessary and excessive force. Stopping at the right time is essential, and goes in your favour. Failing to stop at the right time will weigh heavily against you.

- **Do not automatically attack accomplices**. Every action in a situation must be justified. Just because a second threat was with the first threat at the start of the incident, does not give you the automatic justification to use force against them. This does not mean you cannot; it just means you must be ready to justify any action against any threat.
- **Calling police and ambulance and rendering aid**. If it is safe to do so, consider rendering first aid to the threat(s). To most civilian victims of assault, it will seldom be safe and the necessary action is to flee the scene. However, were you to render aid, this would be compelling evidence of your good intentions and lawful bearing. Once away from the scene, if you run, you must call police and ask for police attendance. Also mention that there are injured parties and that medical

intervention will also be necessary. Remember that all 999 calls are recorded and will form part of the evidence in any subsequent prosecution linked to the incident.

These are just some of the actions you could take. Now you can see that observing the Legal Imperative and **building a lawful justification for the use of force does not have to be left to chance, but can be pro-actively worked towards before and even during the conflict.**

This exploration also should make it clear to you why the time element of the Tactical and Legal Imperatives exists in the way that it does. The earlier you take violent action, the safer you are tactically, but the less safe you are legally. **You are safer because you act before the threat(s). You are in more legal danger because the earlier you act, the less time there is to inject evidence to weigh down your side of the scales.**

Module 8 - Building a Lawful Justification for Use of Force (After Conflict)

In the last module we explored the legal and police processes around responding to violent incidents. In this module, we will explore how to pull all you have learned into a coherent narrative, presenting a competent use of force justification, which will include your reasoning and justification for using force to defend yourself.

Learning Outcomes:

- How to present a competent and coherent Use of Force Justification, presenting all relevant information honestly, calmly, and clearly.

The Contents and Structure of an Effective Use of Force Justification

Tone

It is a general recommendation that when giving an account of an incident, especially one where force was used, one should avoid technical jargon. If you are a martial artist, or well versed in self-defence, do not use the technical terms for your punches and kicks. It adds nothing. Tell the whole truth, of course, but use simple terms. The Law is an adversarial system, and skilled barristers will dismantle you and your argument with ease if you give them an inch. A common strategy for this is to paint trained people as experts and then suggest that any use of force was unnecessary because if they were so skilled, couldn't they have controlled the aggressors without causing harm? In reality, no amount of skill will allow a single person to safely control multiple, hostile and committed threats without significant use of force, but that doesn't stop barristers from suggesting otherwise.

Tell the whole truth, but do it simply, in plain language, as a layman.

Narrative

Clearly, a justification for use of force must take the form of a narrative account of what actually happened.

In practice, the narrative is the vehicle in which all other aspects of the justification are carried. You must begin to lay out the facts about what happened, slowly, and completely, including as much detail as you can remember. If you cannot remember something, you must not lie, nor must you guess as to what happened. Simply state that you do not remember. If your emotional state caused you to lose focus and not be aware of some element of the conflict, state that. Doing so will help build a picture of your fear for the investigator.

Describe Your Attackers and Their Nature

Your narrative must include a description of the people who attacked you, along with their demeanour and any perceived intoxication.

It is vital to state any relevant comparisons between you and the threat(s). We will look at this in more detail in a moment, but for now simply understand that comparisons are an essential part of any force justification. If you are a 90 pound female and you were faced with two 190 pound males, there is clearly a very strong justification for use of force, and earlier in the incident than if you were a 190 pound male facing an unarmed, 90 pound female.

Describe Actions Taken by the Threat(s)

You must include a detailed account of the actions of the threats that preceded the violence they used against you, or, if you were pre-emptive, the actions they took that preceded your pre-emptive use of force against them.

Your account of these actions needs to go into every detail, down to the last step, gesture, word or contact. If you crossed the street and they followed, state that. If you stood still and they took away your distance, state that. Leave nothing out. This is a chance to get in all the points discussed in the previous section.

Describe Actions You Took to Avoid or De-Escalate

You must state, in detail, what actions, if any, you took to prevent, avoid or de-escalate the situation. For example, you would say you walked away from the threats when they approached and you crossed the road.

Often, the narrative will swing between your actions and the threat's actions multiple times as you describe what you did, what they did, what you did, what they did. This is fine, and necessary in order to get everything into the justification that needs to be there. You might consider thinking back to the incident with the concept of 'beats' in your mind. We covered this in Module 2, when we mentioned The Speed of Violence, and it is certainly useful to consider each beat of the conflict individually to be sure you break down everything and miss nothing out.

IMPORTANT: If you live in a 'duty to retreat' jurisdiction, such as Scotland or the USA, you must be sure to state here what you did to attempt escape before resorting to use of force.

Describe What Their Actions Made You Think They Were Going to Do

You must include in your narrative a speculation about what you thought at each stage the threat was going to do. It goes without saying that, at the time, you had an opinion that they were going to do something violent to you. You need to remember what it was you thought they were going to do, and you need to state it as part of your narrative.

"I saw the male coming towards me. His lips were parted and his teeth were bared, like an animal. At that moment I was sure he wanted to kill me."

"I saw the male clench both his fists. Then his right hand went back and I thought he was going to hit me."

These examples demonstrate how important it is to state what you believed was going to happen. Remember the legal definition of a common assault in the United Kingdom:

> "Any act where a person intentionally or recklessly causes another person to apprehend immediate and unlawful personal violence."

This legal definition means that to claim self-defence, you must have apprehended immediate and unlawful violence. In other words, you had to have had an honest and reasonable belief that the threat was going to use violence against you, and you had to have been in fear of that violence. The police, prosecutor, and eventually the court cannot know you had this belief and fear unless you state it in your initial account. You must do so with enough detail that someone else hearing it could easily come to the same conclusion as you about what was about to happen, and what they would have done about it. Remember, you are allowed to be wrong about your assumption of the threat's intent, but your belief has to be honest and reasonable. Your description of events is the largest factor in making investigators see that your belief was exactly that, honest and reasonable in the circumstances.

Describe How Your Belief Made You Feel

You had a belief that the threat was about to punch you in the face. How did that make you feel? Your emotional state — your fear — is a vital component of the justification. You must state this. Do not be afraid to state a fear of secondary consequences too:

"He held an uncapped needle. I thought he was going to stab me with it. I was terrified I would get infected with Hepatitis or HIV. I thought I was going to die."

Leave out the emotional content, and your justification loses its most vital aspect, that of your fear. Once again, the legal definitions mandate that you were apprehending — fearing — immediate and unlawful violence.

Reaching the Threat Threshold

The previous two points — what you thought the threat was about to do, and how it made you feel — are essentially about describing the moment you felt you reached the Threat Threshold but you should consider the Threat Threshold as a separate point so that you can be sure you cover it thoroughly.

Remember, you should not use the term Threat Threshold. Technical jargon is to be avoided. Instead, you must tell investigators as part of your narrative exactly what the attackers did that made you realise you had to use force or face being overwhelmed and injured, or killed.

There are a number of actions that could push you to the Threat Threshold and justify the pre-emptive use of force. Here are a few examples:

"I saw his hand disappear behind him. Suddenly he was holding a knife. I thought he was going to kill me with it. I knew if I didn't do something then he would stab me. I lashed out at him to stop him from stabbing me."

"I saw his fist clench. I knew then that he was going to hit me. I was able to hit him first, and get away."

"The male in front of me was shouting abuse, but not moving. I then noticed his friend walking around the side of me. I thought he was trying to set me up and attack me from where I couldn't see him. I knew if I waited, they would be able to overwhelm me and I was terrified they were going to hurt or kill me. I had to hit the male in front of me. After this, I was immediately attacked by the second male, but because I'd taken the initiative and was moving, I was able to fight this attacker off too."

"Both the threats were twice my size. Their language towards me was disgusting and made me think they were going to sexually assault me. I was panicking. I've never been so afraid. I knew if I didn't do something they would attack and I would have no chance so I kicked the one male in the groin and then managed to kick the second one the same before he could react. Then I ran and called police."

"I saw his eyes bulging, as if they were coming out of their sockets. His teeth were bared. I could see he was intoxicated and very aggressive. His level of aggression told me he was about to become violent, so I acted to prevent that violence."

In all these examples, the victim is describing where the Threat Threshold was, and why they believed it had been reached. Check if you have covered this in the previous components, and if you have not covered it, include it as a separate component of your Use of Force Justification.

What Actions Did You Take to Stop the Threat?

You have already covered what actions you took to try to avoid or de-escalate the situation. Now, if you have used force, you must state what actions you took that made up that use of force. There is no harm in again repeating why you took them at each stage.

In describing your use of force, do not leave anything out. It will not help. If there are cameras and witnesses that will say you kneed someone in the face, and you do not say you did, it doesn't look good. Of course, in the grip of the Acute Stress Response, you may well block out the realities of the traumatic experience. Investigators understand this, and there is no harm in saying you were so afraid that you cannot now remember everything.

Also do not be afraid to say you hit someone as hard as you could, if that is what you did. If your justification is moral and correct, and you threw a punch at a threat you thought was trying to hurt or kill you, of course you hit them as hard as you could. Tell the whole truth. If you were acting morally, and in honest defence of your life or the life of another, you have nothing to hide.

What Did You Think Would Happen if You Did Not Take These Actions?

You may have already covered this, but check and make sure. It goes to build a picture of what you believed was going to happen, and why you were afraid, both necessary components of the justification.

What Happened After the Incident?

Finish your narrative account by explaining what happened after the incident. Include your 999 call, and any attempts you made to render aid. If you are giving the account a few days or more after the incident, also include the long-term consequences you may have experienced in the aftermath, such as anxiety, fear of going out, flashbacks and the like, which all help to paint a picture of the truth of your involvement in the incident, and its effects on you and your life.

A Final Word on Use of Force Justification

If you structure your Use of Force Justification to include the above points, and you were able to follow the dictates of the previous section and lay evidence of right and lawful action before and during the incident itself, you are well on your way to concluding your involvement in the incident without any negative legal consequences.

To conclude our exploration of the law relating to self-defence, I want to bring us back to morality. Earlier we mentioned that there were a triumvirate of considerations that a person must observe in the positive application of force in defence of self or others — lawfulness, tactical soundness and morality. It cannot be stressed enough that to be lawful, and to successfully justify the use of force against another human being, you must act lawfully in the first place, and that lawfulness nearly always follows morality. The nature of conflict and investigation is that it often contains its own checks and balances.

There is no real distinction between the three factors: moral; tactical, legal. The lines between them blur. If there is a tactical consideration in the heat of conflict that led you to believe you were at the Threat Threshold and had a Tactical Imperative to act, that tactical consideration also forms part of your moral and legal justification.

Your tactical justification, then, is your moral justification, and is your legal justification. This is vital to remember, as it underpins all Use of Force Justification.

Module 9 - A Civilian's Guide to the Legal Process That Follows a Violent Incident

This final module examines the processes that may occur after a violent incident, in terms of police response. It is a brief look into a world that most innocent victims of violent crime will never have seen. We have included it here to assist you in remaining calm and communicating effectively should the worst happen and you are arrested following a violent incident where you have used force to defend yourself.

Learning Outcomes:

- Understand the processes that will occur if you are investigated for, and arrested for an offence following a violent incident where you used force to defend yourself.

You have hit someone. It was self-defence. You know that, to the very core of your being. You did everything you could to avoid the situation but it still occurred. A man came to you and threatened your life. You hit him, and his friend. You hit well. They are on the floor, unconscious and unresponsive, bleeding. You have called for police and ambulance. What happens next? Here is a rough account of the order in which things will happen.

1. Police will arrive. Where there has been violence, police will likely be first responders as even when ambulance crews arrive near the scene of a violent incident they often sensibly wait nearby for police to secure the scene before attending.

2. Police will act immediately to make the scene safe. Their first duty of care is not to the injured but to the public at large, by bringing a rapid and controlled end to any violence or aggression. If you are the last person standing, you represent an immediate threat to the officers attending. Remember that at this point they do not know you, or the threats you faced. They do not know the situation, the circumstances, what was said, what was done. All they see is injured people and you stood over those people, the most likely cause of injuries sustained by those injured people. Expect to be loudly and aggressively challenged, ordered back or onto the floor. It is in your immediate interests to comply without hesitation and completely to all instructions given. Being aggressive to police in any way justifies their use of force against you, which puts you and them at risk. Further, it will count significantly against you on the score sheet, tipping the balance of probabilities back in favour of your attackers. How does it look if you are violent or aggressive with police and then claim that nothing was your fault? Comply. Immediately, totally. Explanations are for afterwards.

3. Arrest. If there are obvious injuries to some or all parties it is very likely you will be arrested for the offence of common assault, ABH, GBH, or even a public order offence such as Affray (Section 3 Public Order Act). A police officer will likely handcuff you — again offer no resistance — and state that you are under arrest. They will tell you what the offence is, what their grounds are for believing you have committed that offence, and what the necessity is for your arrest — this will most likely be to prevent further harm by removing you from the scene. You will be cautioned, meaning that whatever you say after the caution is given will have evidential value, and that refusing to answer questions will in itself have evidential value (the court can make an inference regarding your silence — in other words, not answering a question when asked of you may look bad and make the court less likely to believe what you have to say later). It is advisable to say little at this point as you will be shaken and adrenalised, which may impair your ability to think clearly. You might simply say that you were attacked and you feel shocked and need time to calm down. Your compliance will win you sympathy from police in most cases; even where police believe someone to be guilty, they tend to treat people with care and respect, provided respect is shown back. Remember, it is not the job of the police to make judgements or assign blame. That is for the courts. The role of the police is to protect and to investigate, gathering evidence that may be presented at court.

4. Custody. If you have not been arrested you may be told to attend the next day for a Voluntary Interview, or if the situation is so obviously a case of self-defence, you may simply be asked to give a victim statement either on scene or at a later time. Alternatively, if you have been arrested, you will be taken to custody. Do not panic. For someone not used to this process, this can be terrifying, but it is not designed for that effect. It is just process. Arrest exists to bring a prompt and effective halt to any violent or dangerous situation and to allow an investigation to take place. Police are only allowed to hold you for a maximum 24 hours in most cases, and the majority of the time you will not be held this long. You will be taken in and locked in a cell while officers secure witness statements, physical evidence and any CCTV. If you are genuinely and provably innocent, you may be released soon after without interview or further action. However if the injuries you have caused are serious, and/or the situation is ambiguous, you will be required to account for your actions in interview. Again, do not panic. This is your chance to put across your side of the story, and it is the job of the police to listen to your account and to include this in their developing picture of what happened. If the case goes to the Crown Prosecution Service, it won't even be the police who make the decision to charge you; the interview and full case history will go to the CPS Prosecutor for decision. This will all happen within 24 hours of arrival at custody and usually much sooner.

5. Tea. Guilty as sin, or obviously innocent, custody skippers are usually very civilised and obliging if you are civilised with them. Act with decorum and decency and you can count on tea, coffee, water, or even food while you wait for legal advice to arrive and the officers to investigate your incident. Take advantage of this. You want to use the time to relax, as hard as this is to do, and to allow the adrenaline to wear off and exit your system so that your cognitive process can return to its peak. As anyone who has served in the Forces knows, there is nothing like a brew to assist in this process.

6. Legal Counsel and Interview. You have the right to free and independent legal advice. You should always take this opportunity. If you ask for legal counsel you will be given the chance to talk with a solicitor prior to going into interview, and the solicitor will usually accompany you into the interview. Asking for a solicitor does not count against you in terms of you looking guilty; it is part of legal due process. The solicitor is the first person you speak to who is on your side and will listen to your story and help you put together the events in a coherent narrative. If you have acted morally, an interview is a simple process. You simply answer questions honestly, taking care to explain not just what happened but how you felt about what happened at each stage, and what you thought was going to happen to you if you did not act. Remember that you have the legal right to self-defence if you believe that you are going to be harmed. If you have acted in good faith and are honest, this will come across in interview and will be supported by your clean record and should be obvious to the interviewing officer. This is why right, moral action is so important. None of the points in this book will help those who act with ill intent because it is nearly impossible to hide that intent from the investigative spotlight of witnesses, CCTV and trained interview.

Remember that in most cases of self-defence, it is often not what you did but what you say about what you did that matters. The wording of the law is that you may do what you reasonably believe is necessary to defend yourself from the threat in the circumstances as you believed them to be. There is a lot of subjectivity here. It is up to you to convey your emotional state, your level of fear, what drove you to fear such harm that you used force to protect yourself. Spare no detail when it comes to your emotional state. Now is not the time to appear strong and deny you were afraid; it is your fear that will save you. Fear of harm is necessary for a plea of self-defence to be made out.

7. NFA, RUI, Charge. If it is obvious that self-defence has occurred and your use of force is lawful, a decision will likely be made to NFA (release you with No Further Action), and possibly pursue charges against your attackers. In cases of low level assault this decision will be made by police; in more serious cases, it will be made by the CPS. Sometimes, if there is further investigation necessary to determine the nature of the incident, you may be Released Under Investigation. If a decision to charge you is made, this does not mean that you are guilty; it merely means that you will attend court in the matter. If this decision is made, you will either be bailed or remanded.

8. Bail or Remand. Bail means you will be released with certain conditions that must be complied with. Example conditions are not to contact directly or indirectly any other person involved in the case, such as witnesses or the people you harmed, or who harmed you. Sometimes bail may restrict your movements, banning you from entering areas or forcing you to reside at certain addresses. In more serious cases you may be remanded. This means you will be held in custody until you can be put before the court. Your appearance will first be at Magistrates Court, usually the next day unless you were arrested on a Saturday evening, in which case your appearance will likely be on Monday morning. From there a magistrate may order you incarcerated in a prison until you can appear at Crown Court, or they may order you released on Court Bail.

9. Court. Eventually, if you are charged, you will appear before the court. It is here you will make your final stand and it is here that the law of the land will find you guilty of your charge(s) or innocent, or that you are guilty of harming a person but for reasons of lawful self-defence. Everything you have done and said up to this point will now be brought out and scrutinised; again, if you have acted morally and paid attention to your actions with respect to the lessons in this section, there is a good chance that the court will find in your favour. If this is a low level, or summary offence, you will be tried at a Magistrates Court and it will be a bench of Magistrates that decide guilt or innocence. If this is a serious (indictable) offence, the case will go to Crown Court, where a jury will decide the outcome. Either way, much of the work to sway the case either way will have been laid down in the first few hours following the assault and during the assault itself. If you have acted morally and taken note of these lessons, chances are good. If you have not acted in good faith, chances are poor. Somewhere along this process the truth tends to out. That is why it is essential to learn about self-defence strategy, morality and law ahead of time, not when the wheels have come off and violence is upon you. It is too late then to ask the questions and learn the lessons.

Conclusion

As we said at the beginning of this book, no study of self-defence is complete without a thorough understanding of the law. Our objective with Rules of Engagement is to give you this legal understanding, so that you are equipped to defend yourself in the arena of the criminal justice system, just as your physical training equips you to act physically to defend yourself in a violent incident. With Module 9 complete, we have reached the end of the Rules of Engagement syllabus. You should now have a solid understanding of the law as it relates to use of force in self-defence, and be in a position to make good moral and lawful decisions in conflict situations, and defend those decisions after the fact.

If there are any gaps in your understanding, we invite you to contact the Lawful Survival training team at the following address and put your questions to us:

questions@lawfulsurvival.com

Visit www.lawfulsurvival.com and sign up to our email list, to be kept up to date on dates for our seminar series, or simply take the Rules of Engagement On Demand course, which adds a video element to this syllabus.

We also recommend that you pick up the full Lawful Survival book at Amazon, which includes one of the most detailed analyses on the tactics, psychology and law of violence ever written. Lawful Survival also includes a modular training plan for Instructors, so that you can begin to include use of force justification and decision making into your physical training.

Thank you once again for choosing Lawful Survival, and for reading this book. We hope it helps to keep you safe, legally, morally and physically.

Printed in Dunstable, United Kingdom

64267370R00069